Sharks

Great White Shark

by Deborah Nuzzolo

Consulting Editor: Gail Saunders-Smith, PhD

Consultant: Jody Rake, member
Southwest Marine/Aquatic Educators' Association

Capstone
press

Mankato, Minnesota

Pebble Plus is published by Capstone Press,
151 Good Counsel Drive, P.O. Box 669, Mankato, Minnesota 56002.
www.capstonepress.com

Printed in China

102009
005561

Library of Congress Cataloging-in-Publication Data
Nuzzolo, Deborah.
 Great white shark / by Deborah Nuzzolo.
 p. cm. — (Pebble plus. Sharks)
 Includes bibliographical references and index.
 Summary: "Simple text and photographs present great white sharks, their body parts,
and their behavior" — Provided by publisher.
 ISBN: 978-1-4296-1727-7 (hardcover)
 ISBN: 978-1-4296-5041-0 (saddle-stitched)
 1. White shark — Juvenile literature. I. Title.
QL638.95.L3N88 2009
597.3'3 — dc22   2007051312

Editorial Credits
Megan Peterson, editor; Ted Williams, set designer; Kyle Grenz, book designer; Jo Miller, photo researcher

Photo Credits
Bruce Coleman Inc./Maris Kazmers, 19; Ron & Valerie Taylor, 10–11
Getty Images Inc./Minden Pictures/Mike Perry, 7; Photographer's Choice/David Nardini, cover; Science
 Faction/Stephen Frink, 17
Nature Picture Library/Doc White, 14–15
Shutterstock/Simone Conti, backgrounds
SuperStock, Inc./Pacific Stock, 4–5
Tom Stack & Associates, Inc./Dave Fleetham, 9, 13
Visuals Unlimited/Brandon Cole, 20–21; Marty Snyderman, 1

Note to Parents and Teachers

The Sharks set supports national science standards related to the characteristics and
behavior of animals. This book describes and illustrates great white sharks. The images
support early readers in understanding the text. The repetition of words and phrases
helps early readers learn new words. This book also introduces early readers to
subject-specific vocabulary words, which are defined in the Glossary section. Early
readers may need assistance to read some words and to use the Table of Contents,
Glossary, Read More, Internet Sites, and Index sections of the book.

Table of Contents

Fearsome Fish

Great white sharks

are fearsome fish.

They are the largest

hunting fish in the world.

Great whites live worldwide

in mostly cool water.

They swim along the shore

to search for food.

Great White Shark Pups

Great white shark pups

are born live.

Between two and 10 pups

are born at one time.

Shark pups live and grow
on their own.
Great white sharks live
about 25 years.

11

What They Look Like

Great white sharks have white undersides and gray backs. The gray color blends in with the ocean floor.

5 feet (1.5 meters) long

15 feet (4.6 meters) long

Great white shark bodies look like footballs. This smooth shape helps great whites speed after prey.

Great white sharks

have a nostril

on each side of their snout.

They use their sense of smell

to find prey.

nostril

Hunting

Great white sharks hunt

seals, sea lions, and dolphins.

They can jump out of the water

to catch prey.

Great white sharks bite prey
with many sharp teeth.
Few animals can escape
the jaws of this ocean hunter.

Glossary

escape — to get away from

fearsome — frightening or scary

hunt — to chase and kill animals for food

nostril — an opening in a sharks's nose through which it smells

prey — an animal hunted by another animal for food

pup — a young shark

shore — the place where the water meets land; many sharks swim in the shallow water near the shore.

smooth — even and free from bumps

snout — the long front part of a shark's head that includes the nose, mouth, and jaws

worldwide — extending or spreading throughout the world

Read More

Crossingham, John, and Bobbie Kalman. *The Life Cycle of a Shark.* The Life Cycle Series. New York: Crabtree, 2006.

Lindeen, Carol K. *Sharks.* Under the Sea. Mankato, Minn.: Capstone Press, 2005.

Thomson, Sarah L. *Amazing Sharks!* An I Can Read Book. New York: HarperCollins, 2005.

Internet Sites

FactHound offers a safe, fun way to find Internet sites related to this book. All of the sites on FactHound have been researched by our staff.

Here's how:

1. Visit *www.facthound.com*

2. Choose your grade level.

3. Type in this book ID **1429617276** for age-appropriate sites. You may also browse subjects by clicking on letters, or by clicking on pictures and words.

4. Click on the **Fetch It** button.

FactHound will fetch the best sites for you!

Index

Word Count: 157

Grade: 1

Early-Intervention Level: 20